Contents

How to use this book

Each page has a title telling you what it is about.

Instructions look like this. Always read these carefully before starting.

This shows you how to set out your work. The first question is done for you.

This shows that the activity is an **Explore**. Work with a friend.

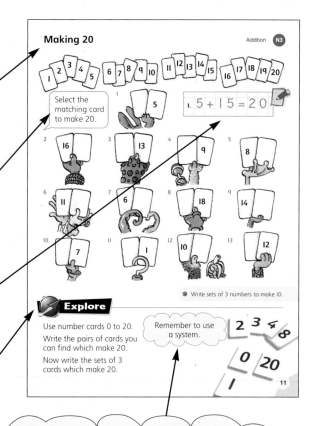

Sometimes there is a **Hint** to help you.

Ask your teacher if you need to do these.

Sometimes you need materials to help you.

Read these word problems very carefully. Decide how you will work out the answers.

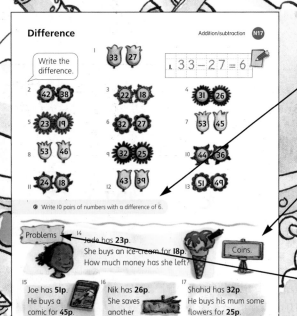

This means you decide how to set out your work.

Write the number made with each set of cards.

1

| 300 |
| 4 | 70 |

ı. 3 7 4

2

| 200 | 8 |
| 50 |

3

| 5 | 30 |
| 100 |

4

| 3 | 80 |
| 600 |

5

| 400 |
| 90 | 1 |

6

| 4 | 40 |
| 800 |

7

| 60 | 500 |
| 9 |

8

| 8 | 50 |
| 900 |

9

| 10 | 2 |
| 400 |

10

| 7 | 200 |
| 70 |

ℯ Write all the numbers in order.

Write the next 4 numbers.

ıı. 2 3 2, 2 3 3, 2 3 4, 2 3 5

11

231

12

144

13

168

14

352

15

419

16

638

17

198

18

897

ℯ Write the 4 numbers before.

Hundreds, tens and units

Here are 100 cubes.

Here are 10 cubes.

Here is a unit cube.

Write how many cubes in each set.

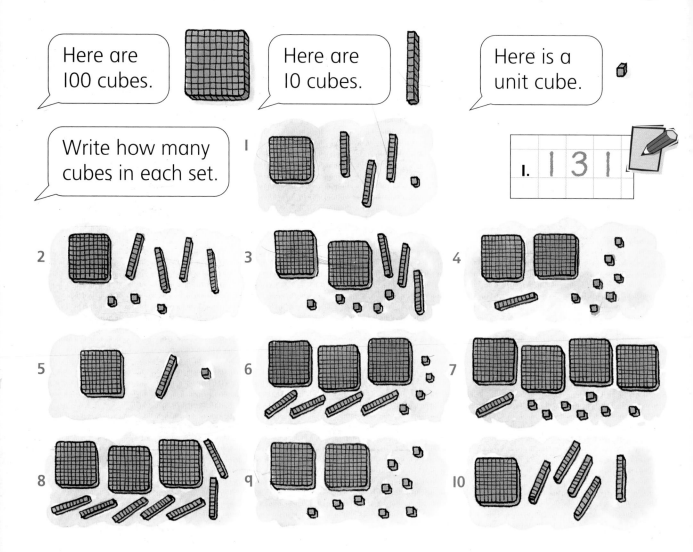

1.

| | 1 | 3 | 1 | |

ℓ Write all the numbers in order.

Explore

Use the cards shown.

Write all the different 3-digit numbers you can make.

Write them in order.

4

Hundreds, tens and units

Write each number in hundreds, tens and units.

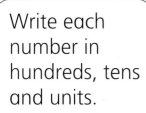

1. 219

I. $200 + 10 + 9$

2  724

3  158

4  366

5  942

6  445

7  222

8  573

9  831

10 787

11  906

12  560

13 700

e Write 5 of these numbers in words.

Write the matching number or number name.

14 Five hundred and twenty-four

14. 524

15 Two hundred and sixty-two

16 Three hundred and four

17 Eight hundred and ten

18 Nine hundred and nineteen

19 Four hundred and twenty-one

20 Six hundred and thirty-nine

21 **188**   22 **707**   23 **220**   24 **888**

Hundreds, tens and units

Place-value **N2**

Count the hundreds, tens and units. Write the total in pence.

1

HTU

1. 3 2 4 p

£1 is 100 pence.

2

3

4

5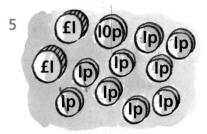

6

7

8

9

10

ℓ Write 10 more and 10 less than each amount.

Draw coins to match each amount.

11. 113 pence

£1   10p   1p 1p
              1p

11 113 pence

12 412 pence   **13** 222 pence   **14** 422 pence

15 106 pence   **16** 330 pence   **17** 602 pence

18 255 pence   **19** 307 pence   **20** 120 pence

6

Hundreds, tens and units

Write each number as an addition.

1. $300 + 80 + 2 = 382$

1
```
300
2    80
```

2
```
500
       8
30
```

3
```
100
      50
```

4
```
5
700
```

5
```
200
70   9
```

6
```
600
       1
20
```

7
```
6
     40
900
```

8
```
400
     4
```

9
```
700
      90
```

Write the value of the red digit.

10   346

10. forty

11   458

12   647

13   812

14   958

15   706

16   460

17   352

18   450

Change the pennies for £1, 10p and 1p coins.

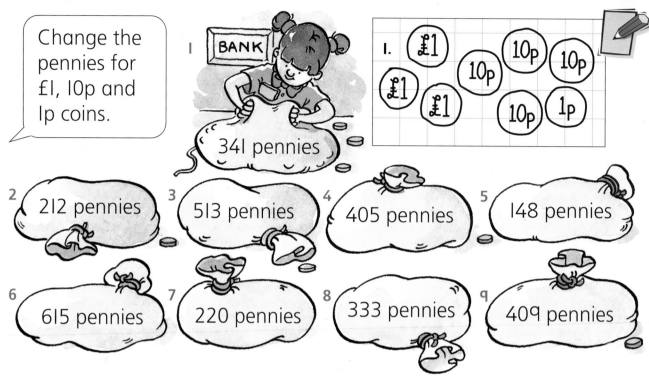

1. BANK
341 pennies

1. £1 £1 £1 10p 10p 10p 10p 1p

2. 212 pennies
3. 513 pennies
4. 405 pennies
5. 148 pennies
6. 615 pennies
7. 220 pennies
8. 333 pennies
9. 409 pennies

Write the totals.

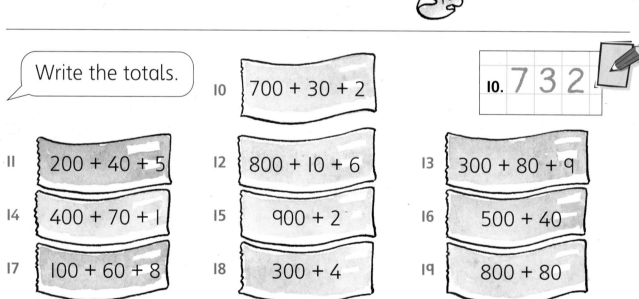

10. 700 + 30 + 2

10. 7 3 2

11. 200 + 40 + 5
12. 800 + 10 + 6
13. 300 + 80 + 9

14. 400 + 70 + 1
15. 900 + 2
16. 500 + 40

17. 100 + 60 + 8
18. 300 + 4
19. 800 + 80

Explore

Use number cards 9 6 4 0.
How many different 3-digit numbers can you make?

Which is the smallest number you can make?

Which is the largest?

9 4 6

6 0 4

Making ten

There are 10 cherries in each group.

How many are inside the bag?

1

I. 7

2

3

4

5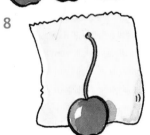

6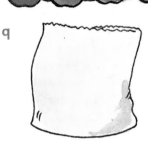

7

8

9

10

e How many to make 20 each time?

Write the missing numbers.

11 8 +  = 10

II. 8 + 2 = 10

12 4 + 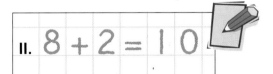 = 10

13  + 3 = 10

14 10 + 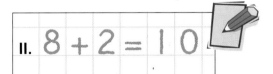 = 10

15 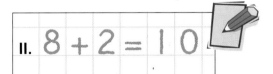 + 2 = 10

16 5 + 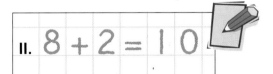 = 10

17 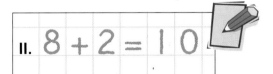 + 1 = 10

18 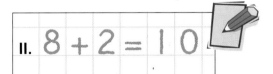 + 0 = 10

19 6 + 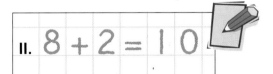 = 10

20 7 + 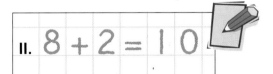 = 10

Making 20

Write how many more cubes you need to make 20.

I

I. $12 + 8 = 20$

2

3

4

5

6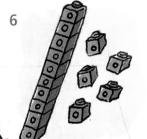

7

8

9

Number facts

| $0 + 10$ | $1 + 9$ | $2 + 8$ | $3 + 7$ | $4 + 6$ | $5 + 5$ |

Write the missing numbers.

10 $8 + $ $ = 20$

10. $8 + 12 = 20$

11 $+ 6 = 20$

12 $3 + $ $ = 20$

13 $2 + $ 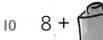 $ = 20$

14 $+ 5 = 20$

Use the number facts to help you.

15 $1 + $ $ = 20$

16 $4 + $ $ = 20$

17 ▢ $+ 7 = 20$

18 ▢ $+ 10 = 20$

Making 20

Select the matching card to make 20.

1. $5 + 15 = 20$

ⓔ Write sets of 3 numbers to make 10.

Explore

Use number cards 0 to 20.

Write the pairs of cards you can find which make 20.

Now write the sets of 3 cards which make 20.

Remember to use a system.

Making 20

Everyone owes Jason 20p. Write how much more money each child needs.

1. $14p + 6p = 20p$

1 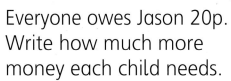 I have 14p.

2 I have 10p.

3 I have 11p.

4 I have 18p.

5 I have 5p.

I have 12p.

6

7 I have 9p.

Each purse needs 20p. Write the missing coins.

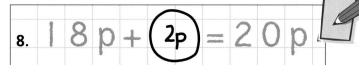

8. $18p + \boxed{2p} = 20p$

8 10p 5p 1p 2p

9 5p 10p 2p

10 2p 2p

11 10p 1p 2p

12 10p 5p

13 10p 1p

14 5p 1p

Adding several numbers

1

Write each score.

I. $12 + 8 + 9 = 29$

Look for tens or twenties.

2

3

4

5

6

7

8

9

10

Copy and complete.

11 $2 + 9 + 8$

II. $8 + 2 + 9 = 19$

Swap the numbers around to help you.

12 $11 + 3 + 7$

13 $14 + 9 + 6$

14 $12 + 9 + 2$

15 $15 + 9 + 5$

16 $15 + 4 + 9$

17 $9 + 4 + 7$

18 $9 + 6 + 3 + 1$

19 $5 + 4 + 10 + 6$

20 $8 + 13 + 2 + 17$

Adding several numbers

Choose 3 items.

Add their prices and write the total.

Write 10 different additions.

$13p + 5p + 6p = 24p$

10p

8p

9p

14p

7p

6p

12p

11p

5p

13p

4p

7p

❷ Choose some sets of 4 items.

Explore

Use number cards 1 to 10.

Find different ways to make 15 using 3 cards.

5 6 3 1

2 10 7

8 4 9

Adding several numbers

Write the fewest coins to make each amount.

I. $10p + 5p + 2p + 1p$

1   18p

2   17p

3   14p

4   21p

5   12p

6   19p

7   24p

8   15p

9   27p

10   13p

11   16p

12   26p

ℯ   Write a different way to make each amount.

Write the number of people on the bus at each stop.

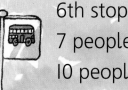

There are 9 people at the start.

?

13   1st stop
3 people **on**

14   2nd stop
8 people **on**
2 people **off**

15   3rd stop
6 people **on**
4 people **off**

16   4th stop
7 people **on**
3 people **off**

17   5th stop
5 people **on**
6 people **off**

18   6th stop
7 people **on**
10 people **off**

Adding to the next ten

Add to each blue number to make the next ten.

1. $6 + 4 = 10$
2. $19 + 1 =$

1	1	2	3	4	5	6	7	8	9	10
2	11	12	13	14	15	16	17	18	19	20
3	21	22	23	24	25	26	27	28	29	30
4	31	32	33	34	35	36	37	38	39	40
5	41	42	43	44	45	46	47	48	49	50
6	51	52	53	54	55	56	57	58	59	60
7	61	62	63	64	65	66	67	68	69	70
8	71	72	73	74	75	76	77	78	79	80
9	81	82	83	84	85	86	87	88	89	90
10	91	92	93	94	95	96	97	98	99	100

How many more pages to the next ten?

11. $37 + 3 = 40$

11
37

12
45

13
23

14
92

15
18

16
76

17
81

Adding

Write the total for each pair of cards.

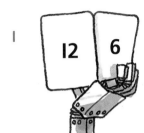

1

1. $12 + 6 = 18$

2

3

4

5

6

7

8

9

10

e Write an addition for each answer to make its nearest ten.

Copy and complete.

11 $15 + 4$

11. $15 + 4 = 19$

12 $17 + 2$

13 $20 + 4$

14 $26 + 2$

15 $48 + 1$

16 $21 + 3$

17 $32 + 8$

18 $51 + 8$

19 $42 + 4$

20 $57 + 2$

Adding

Add 5 to each child's score.

1. $3\,2 + 5 = 3\,7$

1.
32

2. 43

3. 51

4. 64

5. 21

6. 33

7. 72

8. 94

9. 83

10. 44

e Add 5 to each answer.

Explore

Use squared paper.

Write 4 numbers on the cross so that the sum of the red pair and the sum of the blue pair is 25.

Draw five different crosses.

25

24
23 25 2
1

Counting back

Write how much change from 20p.

I. $20p - 4p = 16p$

1. 4p
2. 3p
3. 9p
4. 6p
5. 8p
6. 1p
7. 2p
8. 11p
9. 5p
10. 7p
11. 14p
12. 13p

Count back 5 spaces from each flag.

a. $8 - 5 = 3$

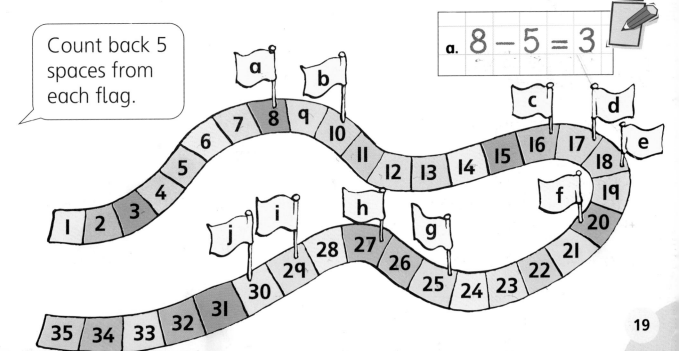

Subtracting

Each ticket should cost 20p. How much must be taken off each price?

1  Cinema 24p

I. $24p - 4p = 20p$

Use coins.

2  School Fete 26p

3  Punch and Judy 29p

4  Dog Show 21p

5  Aquarium 27p

6  Roller Disco 23p

7  Quiz Night 28p

8  Football Match 22p

9  Inflatable Fun 25p

10  Steam Trains 30p

Copy and complete.

11 25p + 5p
    25p − 5p

II. $25p + 5p = 30p$
$25p - 5p = 20p$

12 34p + 6p = ⬚ p
    34p − 4p = ⬚ p

13 42p + ⬚ p = 50p
    42p − ⬚ p = 40p

14 57p + ⬚ p = 60p
    57p − ⬚ p = 50p

15 63p + 7p = ⬚ p
    63p − 3p = ⬚ p

🌐 What do you notice about the pairs of answers?

Subtracting

Write the new price.

1. $27p - 3p = 24p$

2. 3p off 26p

3. 25p 5p off

4. 20p 4p off

5. 47p 5p off

6. 19p 4p off

7. 20p 8p off

8. 35p 4p off

9. 25p 4p off

10. 37p 5p off

Write Tom's and Gita's scores at each stage.   Who is the winner?

?

Tom

11. score 15 — lose 4 points

12. win 15 points

13. lose 10 points

14. win 8 points

Gita

15. score 15 — lose 3 points

16. win 10 points

17. lose 4 points

18. win 12 points

21

Subtracting

> Write the missing numbers.

1. $18 - 3 - 2 = 13$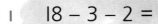

1   $18 - 3 - 2 =$

2   $26 - 1 - 4 =$

3   $19 - 5 - 2 =$

4   $36 - 2 - 1 =$

5   $48 - 5 - 2 =$

6   $26 - 4 - 1 =$

7   $39 - 7 - 1 =$

8   $29 - 5 - 4 =$

9   $48 - 6 - 1 =$

10   $57 - 3 - 4 =$

11   $36 - 2 - 2 =$

12   $28 - 2 - 5 =$

13

Martin has **28p**.
Jez has **7p** less.
How much does
Jez have?

14

Jon has **49p**.
Arran has **8p** less.
How much altogether?

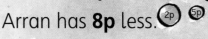

Problems

15

Milly has **15p**.
Meg has **4p** less.
How much does
Meg have?

16

Jason has **5p** less
than Mike.
Together they have **15p**.
How much do they
each have?

Counting in ones

Write the next 3 numbers on each line.

1. 4 8 9, 4 9 0, 4 9 1

1.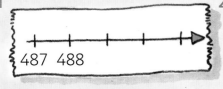
487 488

2.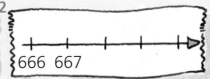
666 667

3.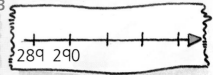
289 290

4.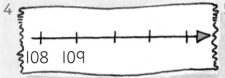
108 109

5.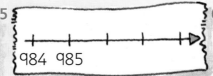
984 985

6.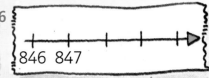
846 847

7.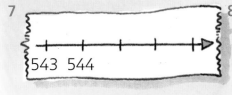
543 544

8.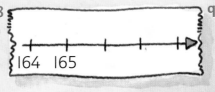
164 165

9.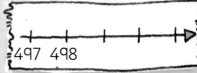
497 498

10.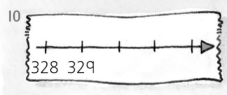
328 329

11.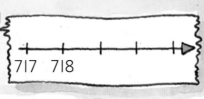
717 718

12.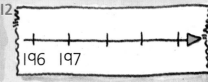
196 197

ℓ Write the 3 numbers before the numbers on each line.

How many spots on each dalmatian?

Guess, then count.

23

Counting back in ones

Copy and complete.

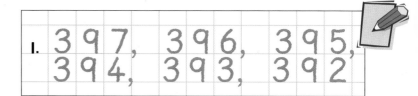

1. 397, 396, 395, 394, 393, 392

1   (397) ○○○ ( ) ○ ( ) ○ ( ) ○ (393)

2   (252) ○ ( ) ○ ( ) ○ ( ) ○ ( ) ○ (247)

3   (812) ○○ ( ) ○ ( ) ○ ( ) ○ ( ) ○ (806)

4   (402) ○○ ( ) ○ ( ) ○ ( ) ○ (398)

5   (105) ○ ( ) ○ ( ) ○ (102) ○ ( )

6   (666) ○ ( ) ○ (664) ○ ( ) ○ ( )

e Make up some bubble trails of your own with missing numbers.

Pink monster is staying in room **302**.

Blue monster is staying in room **203**.

Yellow monster is staying in room **102**.

Hotel

Write the room number 2 rooms to the right, and then 1 room to the left, of each monster.

Write the room number above each monster.

Counting in tens

The children save 10p each week.

How much does each child have after 8 weeks?

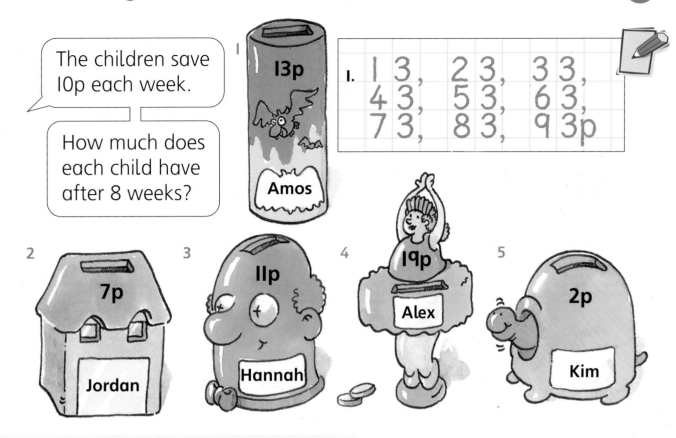

1. 13p — Amos

1. 13, 23, 33,
   43, 53, 63,
   73, 83, 93p

2. 7p — Jordan

3. 11p — Hannah

4. 19p — Alex

5. 2p — Kim

e How much would each have after 10 weeks?

The children spend 10p each week.

How much does each have left after 7 weeks?

6. 84p — Matt

6. 84, 74, 64,
   54, 44, 34,
   24, 14p

7. 89p — Jo

8. 76p — Safa

9. 98p — Jen

10. 95p — Jim

25

Copy and complete the number paths.

1. 100, 110, 120, 130, 140, 150, 160, 170, 180, 190, 200, 210

1 | 100 | 110 | 120 | | 140 | 150 | | 170 | 180 | | | 210 |

2 | 508 | 498 | | 478 | | 458 | | 438 | | 418 | 408 |

3 616, 626, | | | 646, | 666, | 676, | | | | 716 |

4 333, 323, | | 303, 293, | | | | 253, 243 |

5 89, 99, | | | | 139, 149, 159 |

6 111, 121, | | 151 |

Continue each count.

7 | 686 | 687 | 688 | | | | | |

8 | 195 | 194 | 193 | | | | | |

9 | 399 | 400 | 401 | | | | | |

10 | 809 | 808 | 807 | | | | | |

11 | 989 | 990 | 991 | | | | | |

Ten less, ten more

Write the numbers ten less and ten more.

1. 317, 327, 337

327

2. 645

3. 787

4. 838

5. 416

6. 986

7. 212

8. 393

9. 505

10. 900

e Write the number 100 less and 100 more.

Write the missing numbers.

II. 300, 600

11. 100 200 ___ 400 500 ___ ___

12. 150 250 ___ 450 ___ 650 750

13. 370 470 ___ 670 ___ 870 970

14. 510 610 ___ 810 ___ 1010

27

Counting in hundreds

The rockets travel at 100 km a minute.	How far away from the planet is each rocket after 3 minutes?	1. 4 0 0, 5 0 0, 6 0 0 k m

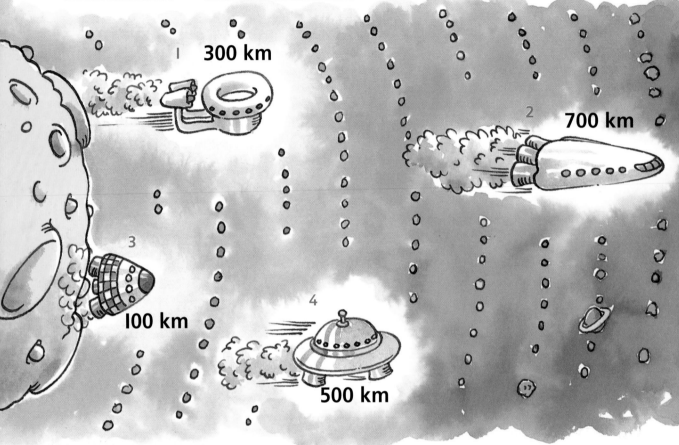

1 **300 km**

2 **700 km**

3 **100 km**

4 **500 km**

Explore

Write a 3-digit number.

Write the number 100 more than your number.

Add the digits of each number.

Compare the totals.

Repeat 8 times.

What do you notice?

1 3 2
1 + 3 + 2 = 6

2 3 2
2 + 3 + 2 =

100 less, 100 more

Write the number 100 less and 100 more.

1.

1. 227, 327, 427

2. 555

3. 218

4. 899

5. 605

6. 310

7. 947

8. 567

9. 409

10. 141

❷ Write the number 1 less and 1 more.

Andi collects football stickers.

Find out her total each month.

January

100 Stickers

122 stickers

February

100 Stickers

She collects another book.

March

She gives away 10 stickers.

April

She collects 30 stickers.

May

She gives away a whole book.

Multiplying

Write a multiplication for each set.

I

I. $3 \times 5 = 15$

2

3

4

5

6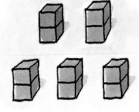

7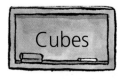

8

9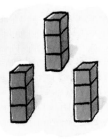

Copy and complete.

Cubes

10. $3 \times 4 = 12$

10	3×4	11	2×5	12	5×3
13	2×10	14	4×4	15	5×2
16	2×7	17	3×6	18	4×5

℮ Double each answer.

Dividing

Write a division for each set.

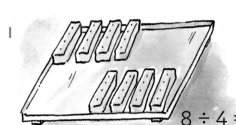

I.

$8 \div 4 = 2$

$8 \div 4 =$

2

$12 \div 3 =$

3

$6 \div \quad =$

4

$15 \div \quad =$

5

$10 \div \quad =$

6

$16 \div \quad =$

7

$\quad \div \quad =$

Copy and complete.

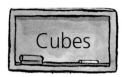

Cubes

8. $8 \div 2 = 4$

8 $8 \div 2$	9 $9 \div 3$	10 $12 \div 4$
11 $10 \div 5$	12 $15 \div 3$	13 $12 \div 2$
14 $20 \div 4$	15 $20 \div 5$	16 $10 \div 2$

Write how many eyes in each picture.

I

1. $5 \times 2 = 10$

2

3

4

5

6

7

8

q

ℯ Double the number of eyes in each picture.

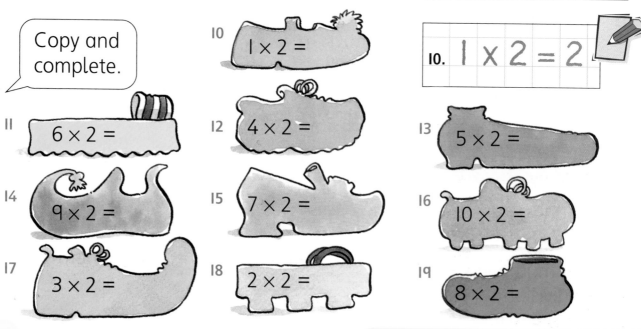

Copy and complete.

10 $1 \times 2 =$

10. $1 \times 2 = 2$

11 $6 \times 2 =$

12 $4 \times 2 =$

13 $5 \times 2 =$

14 $9 \times 2 =$

15 $7 \times 2 =$

16 $10 \times 2 =$

17 $3 \times 2 =$

18 $2 \times 2 =$

19 $8 \times 2 =$

ℯ Write them out in the correct order.

Twos

Josh and Sam collect cans.

They get 2p for each can.

Write how much they get for each group.

1

1. $4 \times 2p = 8p$

2

3

4

5

6

7

8

9

e How much if they get 4p for each can?

Josh spends his money on stickers.

Each sticker costs 2p.

Write how much he spends.

10 4 stickers   10. $4 \times 2p = 8p$

11 7 stickers   12 5 stickers

13 3 stickers   14 8 stickers

15 2 stickers   16 10 stickers

17 9 stickers   18 6 stickers

Twos

Write how many pairs of socks in each box.

i 8 socks

1. 8 ÷ 2 = 4 pairs

2
6 socks

3
14 socks

4
12 socks

5
4 socks

6
10 socks

7
16 socks

8
20 socks

q
18 socks

10
40 socks

Explore

Copy and complete these grids.

Colour the numbers in the × 2 table (2, 4, 6 ...).

Describe the patterns.

Explore for other grids.

MADE IN ENGLAND

Doubling

Write the double shown by each set.

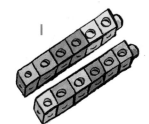

1. double 6 = 1 2

2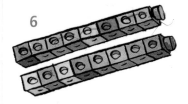

3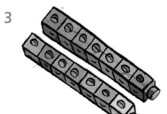

4

5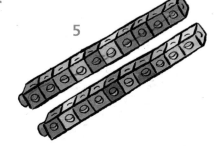

6

7

8

9

e Double each set again.

Darts in the green ring count double.

Write the scores.

10

10. double 4 = 8

11

12

13

14

15

16

Fractions

Copy the shapes.
Colour one quarter.

1

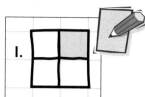

I.

2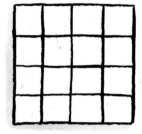

3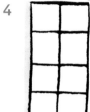

4

5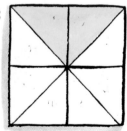

6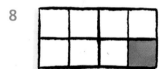

7

What fraction is coloured?
Write $\frac{1}{2}$, $\frac{1}{4}$, or $\frac{1}{8}$.

8

8. $\frac{1}{8}$

9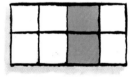

10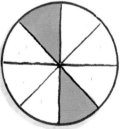

11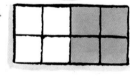

12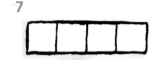

13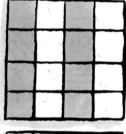

14

15

16

What fraction of each
pizza has been eaten?

17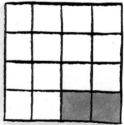

18

19

Fractions

If you ate the fraction of pizza shown, how many mushrooms would you eat?

1

$\frac{1}{4}$ of 8 =

 1. $\frac{1}{4}$ of 8 = 2

2

$\frac{1}{2}$ of 6 =

3

$\frac{1}{4}$ of 12 =

4

$\frac{1}{4}$ of ▦ =

5

$\frac{1}{2}$ of ▦ =

6

$\frac{1}{2}$ of ▦ =

7

$\frac{1}{4}$ of ▦ =

Share the counters equally among 3.

How many counters in each third?

Counters

8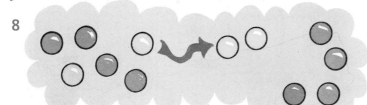

8. $\frac{1}{3}$ of 6 = 2

9

10

11

12

Fractions

Each ribbon is cut into 4 equal pieces.

Write the length of each quarter.

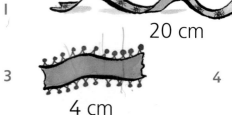

I. $\frac{1}{4}$ of 20 cm = 5 cm

1

20 cm

2

24 cm

3

4 cm

4

8 cm

5

32 cm

6

40 cm

7
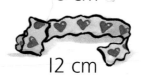
12 cm

Copy and complete.

8   $\frac{1}{3}$ of 6

8. $\frac{1}{3}$ of 6 = 2

9   $\frac{1}{4}$ of 8

10   $\frac{1}{2}$ of 14

11   $\frac{1}{3}$ of 21

Counters

12   $\frac{1}{4}$ of 16

13   $\frac{1}{2}$ of 28

14   $\frac{1}{3}$ of 36

Explore

Copy the grid.

Colour red the numbers that can be split into thirds.

Colour blue the numbers that can be split in half.

Watch out! Some numbers will be red **and** blue.

1	2	3	4	5	6
7	8	9	10	11	12
13	14	15	16	17	18
19	20	21	22	23	24
25	26	27	28	29	30
31	32	33	34	35	36

Counters

Fractions

> Write the missing number.

1. $\frac{1}{\_}$ of 6 = 3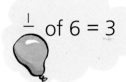

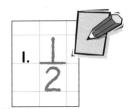
1. $\frac{1}{2}$

2. $\frac{1}{3}$ of = 3

3. $\frac{1}{3}$ of = 5

4. $\frac{1}{2}$ of = 7

5. $\frac{1}{\_}$ of 12 = 4

6. $\frac{1}{\_}$ of 20 = 10

7. $\frac{1}{\_}$ of 12 = 3

8. $\frac{1}{\_}$ of 16 = 4

9. $\frac{1}{2}$ of = 5

10. $\frac{1}{4}$ of = 2

Problems

11. John has **12** biscuits.
He eats $\frac{1}{2}$.
How many are left?

12. There are **16** butterflies in the garden.
$\frac{1}{4}$ are red.
How many are **not** red?

13. Anu sleeps for $\frac{1}{3}$ of the day.
How many hours is she asleep?

14. Mani has **14** cherries.
He eats **7**.
What fraction is left?

15. Mo is **400 m** from the park.
She sprints $\frac{1}{4}$ of the way.
How far does she sprint?

16. There are **24** people on the bus.
$\frac{1}{4}$ are children.
How many are grown-ups?

43

Adding multiples of ten

Write each child's score.

1. $30 + 40 = 70$

I. 30, 10, 20, 40

2. 30, 20, 40, 50

3. 10, 20, 30, 40

4. 60, 30, 40, 50

5. 60, 20, 40, 80

6. 60, 40, 30, 50

7. 60, 40, 30, 50

8. 40, 20, 30, 50

9. 70, 20, 40, 50

The shelf is 100 cm long.

10.
WIZARD EIBO ←30 cm→   DICTIONARY ←40 cm→

Which pairs of objects will fit on the shelf?

10. $30 \text{ cm} + 40 \text{ cm} = 70 \text{ cm}$ yes

11
JUMBO JIGSAW ←50 cm→   ←50 cm→

12
←50 cm→   ←60 cm→

13
←40 cm→   THE HOBBIT ←40 cm→

14
←40 cm→   ATLAS ←50 cm→

44

Subtracting multiples of ten

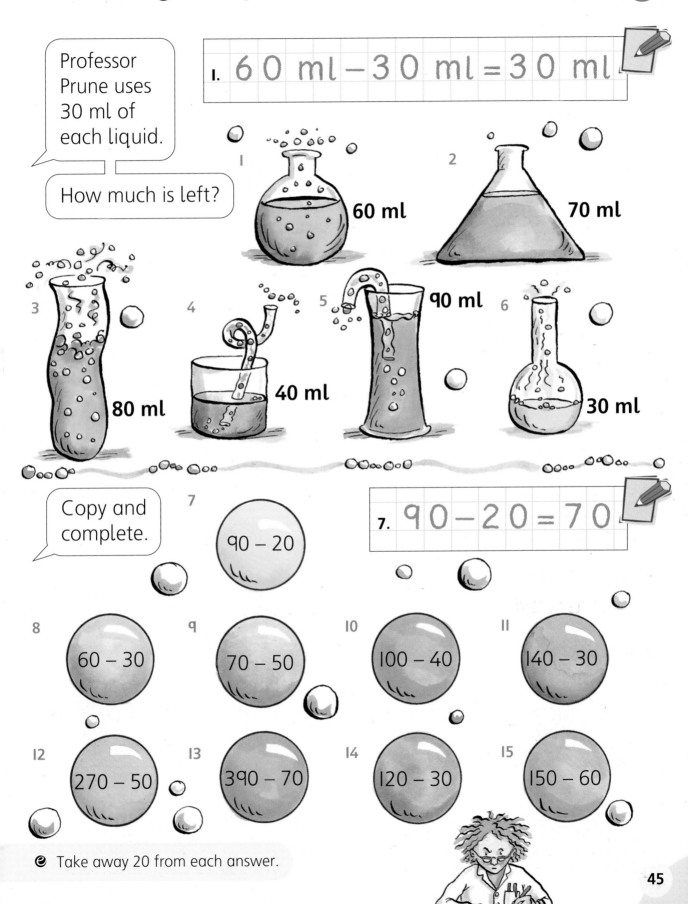

Professor Prune uses 30 ml of each liquid.

How much is left?

1. 60 ml − 30 ml = 30 ml

1   60 ml

2   70 ml

3   80 ml

4   40 ml

5   90 ml

6   30 ml

Copy and complete.

7   90 − 20

7. 90 − 20 = 70

8   60 − 30

9   70 − 50

10   100 − 40

11   140 − 30

12   270 − 50

13   390 − 70

14   120 − 30

15   150 − 60

e Take away 20 from each answer.

45

Adding multiples of five

Write each child's total.

 1   35   20

I. $35 + 20 = 55$

 2   45   15

 3   75   20

 4   65   25

 5   35   35

 6   45   35

 7   65   40

8   85   5

9   75   25

10   55   35

Choose 2 items. Write the total cost.

II. $35p + 25p = 60p$

Choose 6 different pairs of items.

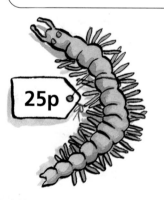

45p

65p

25p

35p

75p

15p

  ℮   Write some pairs you could buy with a £1 coin. Write your change.

Subtracting multiples of five

> Ted needs a new ribbon 30 cm long.

> How much is left from each ribbon?

I. $65 \text{ cm} - 30 \text{ cm} = 35 \text{ cm}$

1  65 cm

2  70 cm

3  45 cm

4  75 cm

5 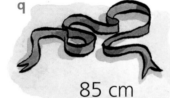 55 cm

6  100 cm

7  95 cm

8  35 cm

9  85 cm

10  105 cm

---

> Each child buys a drink for 25p.

> How much do they have left?

II. $65p - 25p = 40p$

11  **65p**

12  **35p**

13  **75p**

14  **60p**

15  **55p**

16  **85p**

17  **40p**

18 **50p**

℮ They each buy a cake for 10p. Write how much they have left now.

Addition pairs to 100

Match the chains which join to make one metre.

I metre is 100 cm.

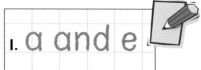
I. a and e

a

50 cm

b

40 cm

c
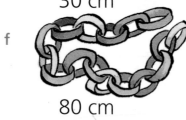
30 cm

d

20 cm

e

50 cm

f

80 cm

g
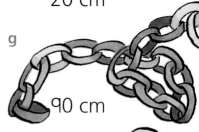
90 cm

h

10 cm

i
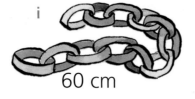
60 cm

j

70 cm

Copy and complete.

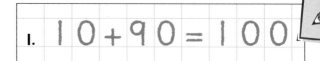
I. $10 + 90 = 100$

1  $10 + = 100$

2 $60 + = 100$

3  $50 + = 100$

4 $15 + = 100$

5 $ + 25 = 100$

6 $45 + = 100$

7 $75 + = 100$

8 $30 + = 100$

q $ + 35 = 100$

10 $ + 5 = 100$

11 $ + 90 = 100$

12 $85 + = 100$

● Write some more missing number additions like these.

One hundred

Write how much of the metre stick has been painted.

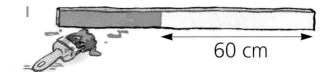

60 cm

I. $100\,cm - 60\,cm = 40\,cm$

2. 30 cm

3. 80 cm

4. 75 cm

5. 45 cm

6. 10 cm

7. 85 cm

8. 15 cm

9. 95 cm

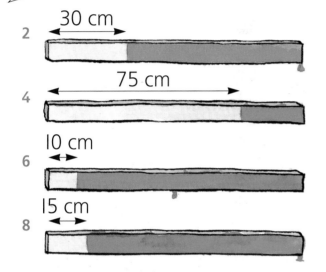

This adult snake is 1 metre long.

10.

10. 65 cm

How much must the baby snakes grow to reach 1 metre?

35 cm

11
75 cm

12
90 cm

13
55 cm

14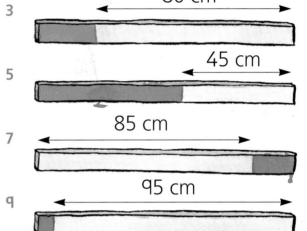
60 cm

15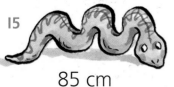
85 cm

16
40 cm

17
5 cm

18
98 cm

e Write how much to reach 1·5 m.

One hundred

How much more to make £1?

I. $55p + 45p = £1$

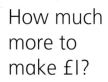  £1 is 100 pence.

1 55p

2 35p

3 25p

4 95p

5 85p

6 70p

7 15p

8 45p

9 65p

10 75p

11 20p

12 5p

e How much to make £2?

Explore

Use nine coins and

five coins.

Use all the coins each time.

Make ten pairs of amounts to total £1.

52p + 48p

Remember to use a system.

Hundreds, tens and units

> Write the number at each arrow.

> Write the number I more.

I. $a = 3\ 1\ 4,\quad 3\ 1\ 5$

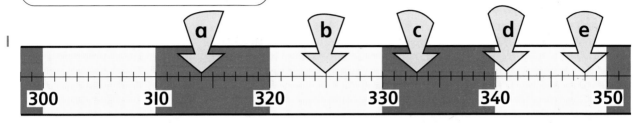

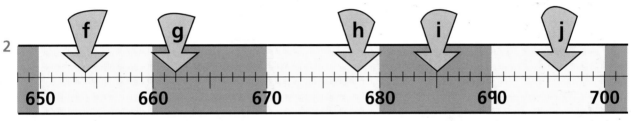

@ Write the number 10 more.

> Write the number I less, 10 less and 100 less.

3

3. $2\ 5\ 5,\quad 2\ 4\ 6,\quad 1\ 5\ 6$

4

5

6

7

8

q

Hundreds, tens and units

Write the number in between.

I 210

212

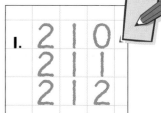

I. 2 1 0
2 1 1
2 1 2

2 476

478

3 907

909

4 316

318

5 278

280

6 100

102

7 899

901

8 400

402

9 330

332

10 222

224

11 831

833

12 510

512

13 601

603

Explore

In between 100 and 200, how many numbers have a 9?

Write them in order.

Do the same for numbers between 200 and 300.

119

139

191

Smallest to largest

Write the numbers on each bunch of balloons in order, smallest to largest.

1 532 210 987

I. 2 1 0
    5 3 2
    9 8 7

2 673 999 402

3 336 372 241

4 560 600 340

5 245 255 325

6 399 299 289

7 778 772 787

8 444 411 441

9 781 178 871

10 110 101 111

Write the largest number and the smallest number.

II. largest 599
     smallest 301

11 412 599 301

12 222 111 444

13 919 819 929

14 602 206 606

15 538 531 536

16 720 757 775

17 360 630 306

18 501 105 150

e Write a larger and a smaller number for each set.

53

Hundreds, tens and units

> Write 2 numbers between these.

> They must be in order from smallest to largest.

1. 4 2 3   4 3 0   4 3 5   4 3 6

1. 423 □ □ 436

2. 400 □ □ 410

3. 770 □ □ 790

4. 555 □ □ 566

5. 328 □ □ 342

6. 204 □ □ 214

7. 787 □ □ 795

8. 696 □ □ 703

9. 508 □ □ 518

10. 256 □ □ 259

Explore

You need: six coins

six coins

six coins.

Use one £1 coin and any other 5 coins.

Write how much you have.

How many different amounts can you make?

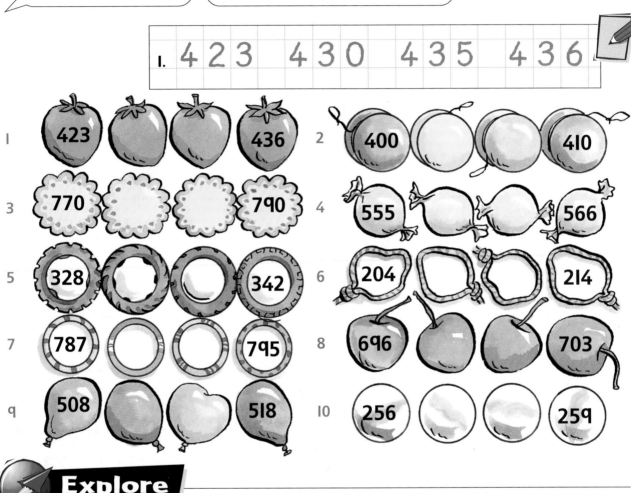

Adding to the next ten

Write the addition pair to make 10.

1

1. $5 + 5 = 10$

2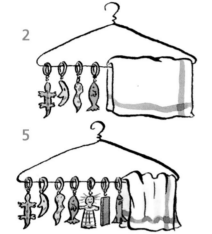

3

4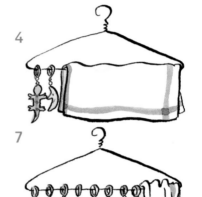

5

6

7

How far to the next multiple of 10?

8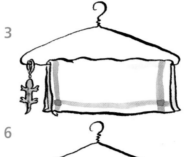

16

8. $16 + 4 = 20$

9 23
10 28
11 37
12 42
13 46
14 55
15 64
16 69
17 74
18 85
19 88
20 92
21 99

1	2	3	4	5	6	7	8	9	10
11	12	13	14	15		17	18	19	20
21	22		24	25	26	27		29	30
31	32	33	34	35	36		38	39	40
41		43	44	45		47	48	49	50
51	52	53	54		56	57	58	59	60
61	62	63		65	66	67	68		70
71	72	73		75	76	77	78	79	80
81	82	83	84		86	87		89	90
91		93	94	95	96	97	98		100

Difference

0   10   20   30   40

Write the difference.

1. **32** **28**   1. $32 - 28 = 4$

2. **43** **36**   3. **52** **46**   4. **24** **17**

5. **52** **44**   6. **41** **36**   7. **35** **29**

8. **26** **15**   9. **32** **26**   10. **45** **37**

50

60

70

Write how much more the tiger cub weighs.

11. 23 kilos   16 kilos   ?

80

13. 28 kilos

12. 33 kilos   21 kilos   17 kilos

90

100

Explore

Two numbers have a difference of 4 and a total of 18.

Which numbers are they?

Make up some more problems like these.

Difference

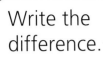 Write the difference.

1

I. $33 - 27 = 6$

2  42 38

3  22 18

4  31 26

5  23 19

6  32 27

7  53 45

8 53 46

9  32 25

10  44 36

11  24 18

12  43 39

13 51 49

℮ Write 10 pairs of numbers with a difference of 6.

Problems

14 Jade has **23p**.
She buys an ice-cream for **18p**.
How much money has she left?

Coins.

15 Joe has **51p**.
He buys a
comic for **45p**.
His aunt gives
him **30p**.
How much money
does he have?

16 Nik has **26p**.
She saves
another
8p.
She buys a pencil
case for **29p**.
She saves **50p** more.
How much now?

17 Shahid has **32p**.
He buys his mum some
flowers for **25p**.
He saves another **40p**.
How much
now?

Subtracting multiples of ten

Write the missing numbers.

1. | 92 | | 72 | | | 42 | |

1. 92, 82, 72, 62, 52, 42, 32

2.

| 96 | 86 | | 66 | | | 36 | | | |

3.
| 98 | 88 | 78 | | | | 38 | | | |

4.
| 91 | | 61 | | | 21 | | |

Each child spends 20p.

How much is left?

5. 84p − 20p = 64p

5. 84p

6. 31p

7. 45p

8. £1·00

9. £1·20

10. £1·30

Adding multiples of ten

More money is added to each money box.

How much now?

1. £1·24 + 30p = £1·54

1 £1·24

2 £1·62

3 £1·79

4 £2·55

5 £3·34

6 £4·15

7 £5·17

8 £8·80

9 £6·43

How much to make £2?

10. £1·40 + 60p = £2

10 £1·40

11 £1·50

12 £1·30

13 £1·70

14 £1·20

15 £1·10

16 £1·75

17 £1·45

e Write how much to make £2·50.

63

Subtracting multiples of ten

Each price has **30p off**.

Write the new price.

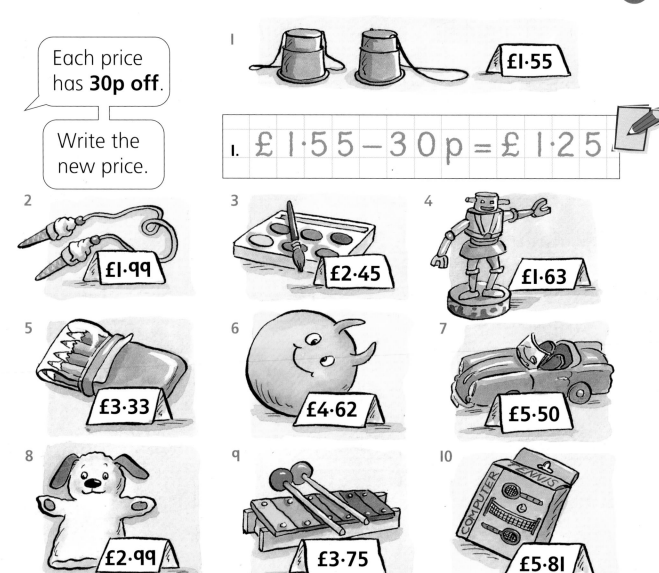

1. £1·55

I. £1·55 − 30p = £1·25

2. £1·99

3. £2·45

4. £1·63

5. £3·33

6. £4·62

7. £5·50

8. £2·99

9. £3·75

10. £5·81

🄴 The next week prices go down another 50p. Write the new prices.

Explore

A shopkeeper has £4·28 in the till.

An hour later he has £5·98.

3 children have bought a toy.

All toys cost either 10p, 20p, 30p, …£1.

Write 5 ways they could have spent their money.

Adding and subtracting

Write the missing amount.

1 £1·12 + { } = £1·22

I. 10p

2 £1·41 + { } = £1·61   3 £1·38 + { } = £1·78   4 £1·29 + { } = £1·49

5 £1·73 − { } = £1·63   6 £1·92 − { } = £1·62   7 £3·16 + { } = £3·36

8 £4·44 − { } = £4·14   9 £5·12 + { } = £5·22   10 { } − 30p = £4·41

---

11 Mena has saved **£3·27**.

Her grandpa gives her **50p**.

How much has she now?

12 Beni bought a notepad for **40p**.

He now has **£2·37**.

How much did he have before?

Problems

13 Jinda has **£1·52**.

She buys a toy for **30p**.

How much has she left?

14 Last week Mark had **£5·21**.

He now has **£5·71**.

How much has he saved?

Adding

Copy and complete.

1 17 + 30 =

I. $17 + 30 = 47$

Use the number grid.

2 37 + 20

3 34 + 40

4 48 + 30

5 29 + 40

1	2	3	4	5	6	7	8	9	10
11	12	13	14	15	16	17	18	19	20
21	22	23	24	25	26	27	28	29	30
31	32	33	34	35	36	37	38	39	40
41	42	43	44	45	46	47	48	49	50
51	52	53	54	55	56	57	58	59	60
61	62	63	64	65	66	67	68	69	70
71	72	73	74	75	76	77	78	79	80
81	82	83	84	85	86	87	88	89	90
91	92	93	94	95	96	97	98	99	100

Add the tens first.

6 56 + 33

7 62 + 23

8 38 + 31

9 47 + 42

10 46 + 23

Choose 2 monsters. Write how much they cost together.

Do this 10 times.

II. $16p + 22p = 38p$

63p

11p

70p

12p

16p

22p

13p

24p

Adding

Add the scores.

1. $123 + 41 = 164$

2.

3. 54

4. 123 54

5.

6. 62 123

7. 130 62

8. 62 126

9. 41 126

10. 135 62

ℓ Write 5 more additions using the snooker balls.

Explore

These children travel in pairs.

Each pair's bags must weigh **less** than 40 kg altogether.

Put the children in pairs.

Annie 14 kg

Mehmet 27 kg

Tim 22 kg

Erin 26 kg

Susie 13 kg

Fred 17 kg

Pinder 24 kg

Marwan 12 kg

Subtracting

Everyone buys a pencil.

Write how much money is left in each purse.

I. £1·45 – 21p = £1·24

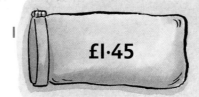
£1·45   21p

2   £2·74   32p

3   £2·55   42p

4   £3·52   31p

5   £1·66   35p

6   £2·38   23p

7   £3·41   31p

Problems

8   **68 nuts**

Sonja Squirrel eats **21** of her nuts.

She finds another **33** nuts.

How many now?

9   **121 nuts**

Sanjay Squirrel finds **42** more nuts.

He eats **51** nuts.

How many now?

10   **136 nuts**

Cyril Squirrel finds **32** more nuts.

He eats **53** nuts.

How many now?

Adding

29 l of petrol are added to each car.

Write the new totals.

I

1. 3 2 l + 2 9 l = 6 1 l

2
44 l

3
25 l

4
29 l

5
34 l

6
68 l

7
77 l

8
48 l

9
53 l

10
36 l

e Add 19 l more to each car. Write the new totals.

Explore

Choose a blue and a yellow card.

Make a 2-digit number.

Swap the digits to make a new number.

Add the 2 numbers.

Do this for some other 2-digit numbers (31, 24 ...).

What do you notice?

3 4 + 4 3 =

Adding and subtracting

> Write the missing numbers.

1   $15 + \{\} = 34$

1. $15 + 19 = 34$

2   $18 + \{\} = 47$ 3 $22 + \{\} = 61$ 4 $45 - \{\} = 26$

5   $32 + \{\} = 71$ 6 $78 - \{\} = 49$ 7 $27 + \{\} = 66$

8   $99 - \{\} = 70$ 9 $16 + \{\} = 65$ 10 $83 - \{\} = 44$

e Write some of your own missing number additions and subtractions.

Problems

11   Jane has **150 ml** of juice. She gives her **2** friends **39 ml** each. How much is left?

12   Mum has **250 cm** of ribbon. She cuts **49 cm** for each of the twin's hair. How much is left?

13   Trevor has **£3·32**. He saves **29p**. How much does he have now?

14   Tien runs **158 m**. Denise runs **49 m** more. How far does Denise run?